ME IN AMERICA

ME

IN

AMERICA

POEMS BY

KELVIN PARKER

Cover Design by Dissect Designs

ISBN 978-1-7355718-0-5 (Hardcover)
ISBN 978-1-7355718-3-6 (Paperback)
ISBN 978-1-7355718-2-9 (eBook)

Library of Congress Control Number: 2020915284

Printed in the United States of America

*For everyone that has ever felt left out, forgotten,
unimportant, and unheard.*

This is for you.

I am America. I am the part you won't recognize. But get used to me. Black, confident, cocky; my name, not yours; my religion, not yours; my goals, my own; get used to me.

— Muhammad Ali

CONTENTS

PART III: WHAT I WANT THEM TO SEE

ME IN AMERICA

When "me" is misrepresented in America,
we are left to find
me in homeland
me in surname
me in amendments
me in freedmen
me in movements
me in reformed
me in disenfranchisement
me in media
me in commentary
me in defamed
me in menace
me in madmen
me in fearsome
me in alarmed
me in unarmed
me in framed
me in crime
me in imprisonment
me in tamed
me in membership
me in unwelcomed
me in resume
me in employment
me in demeanor
me in measured
me in judgment
me in blamed
me in shamed
me in tormented
me in unemployment
me in income
me in homeless
me in impoverishment
me in meaningless
me in remember
me in overcame

INTRODUCTION

Give me your tired, your poor,
Your huddled masses yearning to breathe free,
The wretched refuse of your teeming shore.
Send these, the homeless, tempest-tost to me,
I lift my lamp beside the golden door!

— Emma Lazarus, "The New Colossus"

The inviting voice of America, as described in Lazarus's famous poem, is inscribed on the pedestal of the Statue of Liberty and deeply embedded in our country's consciousness. But the idea of America as a benevolent and welcoming figure is fictional; in truth, Lady Liberty speaks a contradictory message. For some, America speaks of dreams; for others, America only taunts with nightmares. This is a country of wealth and hope, but also one of poverty and despair. Some thrive in its promised liberty. Some fight to survive in its fear. Some soak up its abundance. Some only know its abandonment. Those who are lucky live well and die at peace. Others die while living. Some are called American. Some are classified as other, or nothing.

The America we experience is largely dependent on the identities we hold. If you're white, you're protected with the armor of privilege and access. If you're Black, your life is a long road blocked with obstacles, trip lines, and dead ends. The obstacles are relentless, as racism shows its face in the criminal justice, education, and healthcare systems. The trip lines are violent, with incidences of police and white supremacist brutality. The dead ends are irreversible damages – a loss of hope, internalized self-hatred, and generational trauma.

As Black Americans, we must constantly reaffirm our identity, adjusting ourselves to deflect from negative stereotypes that restrict our access to the "American Dream." As soon as we prove one stereotype wrong, we're met with another. My experience as a Black man is a testament to this. If I'm not an "angry Black man," then I'm arrogant and uppity. If I'm not a thug, then I'm accused of trying to be white. If I'm not lazy, then I'm a threat. If I'm not American, then I'm African American.

As a consequence of racial stereotypes, we as Black people adopt masks for our survival, disarming our blackness to make others feel comfortable and safe in their own insecurities. We hide our pain to appear unaltered and strong.

We live while trying to reconcile two identities: who we are as Black people and who we are in the eyes of American society. Civil rights activist and scholar, William Edward Burghardt Du Bois, or W.E.B. Du Bois, calls this phenomenon double consciousness, "It is a peculiar sensation, this double-consciousness... One ever feels his twoness, – an American, a Negro; two souls, two thoughts, two unreconciled strivings; two warring ideals in one dark body."[1]

Double consciousness explains the dueling nature of the Black American identity and our constant awareness that we are defined by society. Double consciousness leaves us asking ourselves, "Who am I?" But once we answer that question, we find ourselves back in the trap of trying to convince the world to accept us. If we're lucky, some will accept us, but most will never treat us as equal.

WHAT TO EXPECT

Me in America is a collection of poetry that speaks to this conflicting reality. It navigates what it means to be an American for people who look like me. It's also the story of my own lived experiences as a Black man in this country.

In Part One, I reveal aspects of my childhood, bringing attention to adverse childhood experiences (ACEs) that Black children disproportionally face. ACEs are traumatic events and incidences of maltreatment such as physical, sexual, or emotional abuse. "Just under half (45 percent) of children in the United States have experienced at least one ACE."[2] But white children do not experience ACEs at the same rate as their Black counterparts.

According to Child Trends, a nonprofit, nonpartisan research center that studies children at all stages of development, "Nationally, 61 percent of Black non-Hispanic children and 51 percent of Hispanic children have experienced at least one ACE, compared with 40 percent of white non-Hispanic children..."[3] The Child and Adolescent Health Measurement Initiative (CAHMI) reports that "Black children are disproportionately represented among children with ACEs. Over 6 in 10 have ACEs, representing 17.4 percent of all children in the US with ACEs."[4] This is because ACEs also include neglect as a result

---

1   W.E.B. Du Bois, The Souls of Black Folk (New York: New American Library, 1903), 45.
2   Vanessa Sacks and David Murphey, "The prevalence of adverse childhood experiences, nation-ally, by state, and by race or ethnicity," Child Trends, Feb 12, 2018. https://www.childtrends.org/publications/prevalence-adverse-childhood-experiences-nationally-state-race-ethnicity
3   "Sacks and Murphey, "The prevalence of adverse childhood experiences..."
4   "A national and across-state profile on Adverse Childhood Experiences among U.S. children and possibilities to heal and thrive," CAHMI, Oct 2017. https://www.cahmi.org/wp-content/uploads/2018/05/aces_brief_final.pdf

of racism, poverty, oppression, and other social inequities that target Black communities harshly. ACEs have lasting effects on a Black child's well-being, quality of life, and health.

In Part Two, I blend events from American history and personal experiences to bring attention to the origins of racism and how it haunts Black people from youth to adulthood.

Part Three is about healing from the emotional trauma of childhood while trying to figure out how I fit in America. This dynamic is complicated by the addition of new adult traumas in the face of racism and discrimination. Though this section is about adverse experiences, there are also poems about love, loss, and the beauty and struggle of relationships. While these poems may seem out of place, they affirm our humanity as Black people.

Often times, when we hear stories about Black women and men being victims of racism, police brutality, and mistreatment, the news coverage focuses more on the episodes of violence rather than the full lives of the victims. This further dehumanizes us, as we become defined by what we go through rather than who we are.

Black people have dreams, desires, goals, and feelings. We are not objects to be admired for sexual fetishes. We are not a subset of humans to be treated worse than animals. We are not shooting targets to be aimed at. Our stories of joy and love are just as important as our stories of oppression. We deserve to feel the relief of happiness and belonging, especially right now.

Me in America is a tribute to all Black experiences – both the hard and the triumphant ones. It's a celebration of how far we've come and an examination of how far we have left to go. It's a catalog of hurt, sorrow, empowerment, and courage. The book is also a source of education for those outside of the Black community. The poetry gives valuable information on the history of oppression, racism, and inequality in this country. *Me in America* is meant to reach you, no matter your race.

This book is my gift of inspiration and healing to you. Though oppression in America is a challenge, it's a challenge we can, and must, face together.

WHAT
THEY
WON'T
SEE

PART I

CONJOINED TWINS

Born as a pair of conjoined twins,
Prejudice, we seem eternally attached –
Two distinct beings merged by misperception,
With two heads and two necks side-by-side,
Connected to a wider than average torso,
From which extends two arms and two legs.
We each control half of the body
And are free to carry out separate actions,
But we must function in sync with each other
To perfectly coordinate every movement,
Working twice as hard to perform daily tasks
In order to appear normal and less a novelty.
Every decision requires a shared consensus –
Life choices about me become a vote on us.
We have double internal organs, including
Two hearts that yearn for different desires,
Mine longs for love, yours clings to hate;
Two brains that create alternate realities,
Mine shaped by curiosity, yours distorted by fear;
And two sets of lungs that take in the same air,
Yet transfer opposing oxygen into our bloodstream,
Mine brings in hope, yours pulls in doubt.
We are polar opposites fused into one form –
Intricately bound by a social contract
Signed under fear and duress.
Now with our fates forever forged,
Forming a multidimensional bond –
A fragile political alliance for peace
Hinged on willful ignorance –
Our pledged allegiance for unity
Passed along like copies of a chain letter.
We are linked by emotional complicity,
Securely fastened to an understated history
Interlocked with decades of oppression –
The pressure bending us closer together
Like looped metal coils ready to be welded.
We are each other's lifelong nemesis,
Inseparably joined by circumstance –
Tied to an identity measured against the other.

THE INHERITANCE

Some inherit wealth.
    Some inherit an entitlement
to a lavish estate with a gated

driveway and surrounded by
    gorgeous, green landscape.
Some inherit access to a trust fund.

Birth is a coronation for a
    life of privilege, entry to a
backdoor for opportunities

accrued from 400 years
    of using lives for cheap labor.
Some inherit generational pain,

an endowment immediately
    set up after birth, with emotional
trauma disbursed over the course

of their childhood and a lump
    sum of struggles paid once they
reach the age of maturity.

Some inherit a subhuman status.
    Instead of being treated as people,
they are called a "gorilla" and "ape."

Some inherit bruises on the soul
    passed down from one generation
to the next like a sacred language.

Birth is an inauguration to a
    lifetime of economic challenges
and unjust impoverishment

like filling used plastic jugs with
    water taken from a gas station spigot
and then boiling it just to bathe.

The pursuit of happiness
    is a constant struggle for survival.
The quest for the American Dream

is unwillingly diverted to a
    tiresome scavenger hunt for equality.
Some inherit ancestral burdens

and are heirs to indignities.
    Instead of being left assets,
they are beneficiaries

of refurbished identities
    stripped from any tribal connection.
Instead of being left property,

they are in line of succession
    to acquire a fragmented citizenship
in a country that once classified

them as property. Some inherit the
    misfortune of being born free but
die fighting for their lives to matter.

FINDING MOMMY

Mommy, I'm here. Look at me!

Mommy, where did you go?
Mommy, I didn't feel you.
Mommy, is that you?
Mommy, where did you go?
Mommy, where are you?
Mommy, are you coming back?

Mommy, I'm here. Look at me!
Mommy, I'm here. Look at me!

Mommy, what happened?
Mommy, did you notice I left?
Mommy, why didn't you stop me?
Mommy, will you miss me?
Mommy, will you stop?
Mommy, who are you?

Are you my mommy?

WHEN A MOTHER'S LOVE IS TRANSACTIONAL

When a mother's love is transactional,
She will pawn your video games.
Each week she will say, "I will get them out."
Weeks will turn to months,
Months to a year,
And you will eventually realize:
She lied.
You stop asking.

When a mother's love is transactional,
You will understand
The broken promise to you
Was only collateral
For cash to her,
And she will never acknowledge
It wasn't just your
Belongings she forfeited.

When a mother's love is transactional,
You will learn
At a very young age,
Mommy cannot be trusted.
You must hide
Your valuables.
If she finds them,
She will take them.

When a mother's love is transactional,
You will detach from material things.
You will reluctantly
Accept Christmas gifts
From relatives and charities.
You will watch other children
Open presents with their mother
And wonder why she's not there with you.

When a mother's love is transactional,
You will have to give up playtime
For constant downtime.
You will obey mommy's orders
To stay in the house

While she is out,
And you don't ask where
Because you already know.

When a mother's love is transactional,
You will be left to raise yourself
And your younger siblings.
You will substitute your innocence
With premature maturity
To make up for her irresponsibility.
You will learn how to change a diaper
Shortly after the training wheels are taken off.

When a mother's love is transactional,
Neglect will be her only currency –
The medium of exchange
For your needs.
And since you are a child
And she is your mother,
You will instinctively
Accept her payment method.

When a mother's love is transactional,
She will send you Disappointment
As a form of rebate
On your happiness.
You will redeem it every time
You expected her to show up,
But noticed she isn't there for you,
Again!

When a mother's love is transactional,
You will be assigned homework to read aloud
For 10 to 20 minutes under her supervision.
And after you are finished, she will need to
Sign confirming the task was completed.
But she will not be home,
So you will have to learn her signature
And sign it yourself.

When a mother's love is transactional,
She will write you a blank check
Of chronic absenteeism.

She will miss special moments
And important milestones in your life –
Your first school days, your recitals,
Your award ceremonies, your sports games,
Your birthdays, and your graduations.

When a mother's love is transactional,
She will charge you interest for her time.
You will work extra hard for her attention.
You will be an honors student
And selected to give a commencement speech.
You will look out into the audience,
And like so many times before,
You will not see her there.

The price for her love
Will be too high for you to afford.

TRAUMA FROM MAMA

Discouragements

are like

termites –

            they   eat

away

        at

                   your

      confidence

  over

                      time.

SIBLING RIVALRY

In the middle of the night,
    She would leave us
To go tend to him.

When he cried out to her,
    She gently rocked him
Until the thrill fell asleep.

When he woke back up,
    She cradled his urges
Around the clock.

Although he wasn't real,
    She treated him as if
He was our brother.

CUSTODY EXCHANGE

When I was 10 years old,
  a judge disqualified my mom

    from the race and ordered her
  to pass the baton to my dad,

but he wasn't paying attention
  and dropped it during the handoff.

    Instead of him quickly retrieving it
  and sprinting to make up for lost time,

he decided to drag his feet and jog.
  So, I took his place in the race

    and paced myself to jump
  over the hurdles ahead of me.

EMERGENCY CALL

Child neglect
Is like having
Your emergency call
Picked up with no response.
You can hear
Someone breathing
On the other
End of the line,
Listening to your cries
But providing no help.
Your doctor's appointments
And routine checkups
Will not be booked
And your sicknesses overlooked.
You cannot see clearly
And need glasses.
You know something
Doesn't feel right.
You need to go to the ER.
You can barely breathe.
You are just a child.
You need help.
Your doctor's appointments
Continue going unbooked.
Because it's an emergency,
You book the appointment
Yourself.
You go and try to
Fill out the patient form
Yourself.
They ask, "Who is your emergency contact."
You think,
I guess it's me.
They ask for your parents'
Medical history.
I don't know…I wish they
Would just help me.
I don't know…can somebody
Please just help me!

PEDOPHILIA

When it started, abstract ideas cased my brain activity like scavengers
searching for leftovers. Fear presented itself as a casual entity. Denial
wiretapped conversations I had with warning signs. Kind gestures convinced
my premature mind everything was fine. Antonyms for the common good
were mistaken as synonyms I misunderstood. When it happened, my skin
wrinkled like folded paper, and I could only predict what was to come later.
My pulse started throbbing like a scratched CD and caused my heart to skip
a beat. I wondered what would happen to me. Then, letters attacked
like parasites feeding on dead flesh! Vicious terms spelled out my
fate, and I realized I was awake. Creatively, words formed a
meaning that pushed me off a summit, and my life was
immediately ended. When it stopped, hurt passed
slowly like a thunderstorm. My flesh, as if it were
jeans, started to fade to an unrecognizable
shade. Blood began flowing out my body
like ink from a pen, and my corpse was
left lying on a puddle of pages and
buried between the lines of deep,
metaphorical phrases, and
waiting for someone to
make the discovery
of how my soul
was taken by
poetry.

AFTER A CHILD'S INNOCENCE IS TAKEN

After a child's innocence is taken,

he still is just a child,

he still has school to attend,

he still has to walk into class like nothing happened,

he still has homework to complete,

he still has chores to do,

he still has an entire life before him,

he still has to grow up,

he still has life lessons to learn,

there is no time to pause and rest,

there is no moment to cope,

there is no one for him to call out to for help,

he will have to overcome it alone,

but he is still just a child.

DIALOGUE WITH DESTINY 1

Me:
I hate it here, no one cares about me –

Destiny:
My child.

Me:
Huh!

Destiny:
My child, no need to be afraid.
Adversity may have birthed a boy,
But resilience
Will raise a warrior.
Absorb the pressure
From life's challenges
To build momentum –
Redistribute pain to passion,
Convert hardship to creativity,
And reframe your mind
To bring meaning to your name.

Me:
Who are you?
And I'm not a child…
I'm a teenager.

Destiny:
I am Destiny.

Me:
Ha! Destiny?
So are you like one of those things…
One of those…
My fairy godmother?

Destiny:
Hmm.
Yes, you can call me that.
I am here to let you know
Your circumstance

Is a self-extinguishing wick.
But don't worry, little one.
There is a metal bottom
To someday bring you peace.
The world can be a cold,
Dark place, though.
Only passion
Will keep you warm
And be your glare of light
When your days are dim.

Me:
Umm…okay.
Ha.
Why should I trust you?
My mama said don't talk to strangers.
And how do I know you won't
Leave me like everyone else?

Destiny:
No, dear.
I will be here.
I'm no stranger.
I've always watched over you,
Guiding you through this life,
And I will escort you to the next.
We will be together,
Always.
I promise.

Me:
I hate it here.
Let's just go to the next now.

Destiny:
Sorry, it's not time right now.
You have to keep going.
Your dreams are waiting for you.

Me:
I can't do it.
I don't know how.
And I don't have any dreams.

Destiny:
You already did it.
Your dreams will soon find you.
Don't worry.
You have them.
You just have to believe.

Me:
I did?

Destiny:
Yes, I see your present
With one face and two eyes.
I can see what is
And the other what could be.
I want you to dream
Even when the world
Shows you a nightmare.
That is how
You will make it through life.
You will taste defeat
But swallow success.
You will touch failure
But hold on to hope.
Today's pain
Will slowly burn out on its own.
Sleep now, little one.
And don't worry.
I will be here when you awake.

WHAT

THEY

DON'T

SEE

PART II

AMERICA'S SECRET DRESS CODES

If I could go back and talk to my younger self, I would warn him about the challenges ahead of him. I would tell him there's no way to cover the target on your back. It's there simply because of the color of your skin. I would tell him that woven intricately in the fabric of America are a set of centuries-old beliefs codified in the laws governing how you will be forced to participate. That instinctively learned and culturally sublimated, these prefabricated codes have already determined who are treated as legitimate citizens and afforded civil liberties. That freedom is fashionable, merely an artifact of society's political and economic developments – an abstract hieroglyph of time. I would give him the talk his dad won't have with him. I would tell him about America's Secret Dress Codes.

Code <We the People>

On March 6, 1857, the Supreme Court made one of its worst decisions in Dred Scott v. Sandford case by ruling constitutional rights are stylistic details designed only for white people. Encoded in the decision was a principle that any rights extended to Black people must be regarded as faux, branding you as un-American. It's not your fault, we did nothing wrong. These doctrines have been stitched through generations and are fashioning the isms – racism, classism, colorism, separatism, and sectarianism – destroying America's democracy today. These blemishes are but a glimpse of the nation's naked truth and not a reflection of you.

"We" was never meant to consider all, especially people like you, and the Constitution is an embellished costume our founders dressed the country in to disguise a lie. All are free to wear liberty but only "We" has the right to show it. Everyone like you are expected to keep the undergarment covered.

Code <Except As>

The nature of laws is to be transient. They are not enacted simply for the sake of order or progress but an attempt to make the country's lie appear true. For every amendment passed and added to America's ensemble, there are decorative details to complement the look and cover up a dirty stain.

Ratified on December 6, 1865, the 13th Amendment abolished slavery. It appeared to solve the country's sartorial problem.

But if the dress norm previously set was that only white people could ever have and display freedom, appearance management is social and racial control.

Like cording sandwiched between two layers of fabric, inserted in the details of the amendment is a clause ending slavery "except as punishment for a crime" and transmuting it into something else, oppression, a sign language for enslavement for people like you. The style of injustice evolved, but the visual remains the same. Those who know how to dress it up have figured out how to still profit from slavery while acting in accordance with social norms.

Code <Stand Your Ground>

Since "We" was never meant to consider all and freedom came with a clause, then it would make people like you violate social norms just by default. You will be labeled as a deviant. Your mere presence will be perceived as a breach of an unspoken rule of how one should look to be accepted as an American. Instead, they will see people like you as incompatible, nonconforming, and incompliant; thereby, subject to a penalty of imprisonment or death.

On April 26, 2005, the country's first Stand Your Ground bill was signed into law as an enforcement measure for social order. This law implicitly marked you as a human shooting target if perceived as a threat, an idea dating back to the early 1600s known as the Castle Doctrine. It's a principle that defines a man's home as his castle. He has a right to defend his life with deadly force, if necessary, when an intruder enters his home.

But since "We" was never meant to consider all and freedom came with a clause, America was never to be home to Black people. And some will label you as an intruder inside a home where you don't belong and see you as an imminent threat to face deadly force.

But you don't have to live in fear. You don't have to fit in. You can just be yourself. The dress codes created are to make you overdressed for oppression and underdressed for freedom.

You are good enough. It's okay to just be yourself.

DIALOGUE WITH DESTINY 2

Destiny:
Wait, before you leave
And meetup with Independence,
It's time I show you how to blend in.
You can't step out as yourself.
You must learn to be you
And someone else.

Me:
There you go talking in riddles again.
Someone else?
I am me.

Destiny:
This is serious.
Up to now,
Life has reflected
A mirror image back at you.
In your hometown and schools attended,
You have seen faces
That mostly look like yours.
The vantage point is about to change, though.
Your best has brought you this far
But soon it won't be enough
To separate you from the rest.
Soon you will see that your version
Of you in your hometown must be different
Than your version of you in America.

Me:
Umm…I don't get it.

Destiny:
I know.
Don't worry.
I brought you this
To make your transition easier.

Me:
Umm…what is that?

Destiny:
It's a mask for your protection.

Me:
Heck naw!
Protection?
You're kidding me, right?

Destiny:
No…trust me.
First, let's fit the prosthetic to your face.
Have a seat here.
Try it on.
Yes…that's it.
Make sure it lines up with your nose
And check the fit
At the corner of your eyes.
Mmhm.
Apply adhesive glue
To the entire nose area.
Quickly mold it in place
While the glue is still wet.
Once the fit is right
Give it a good, firm press.
There you go!
Now, apply adhesive
At the inside corners of your eyes
And around your brows.
Yes…just like that.
Press, then repeat the same steps
On your forehead.
Good!
Continue down the center of your face,
Beneath your nose,
Around your upper and lower lips,
And your cheeks.
You're doing so well!
Now, carefully apply it to your cheeks.
Almost done.
But to make it appear more realistic,
Paint a smile over the smirk
And meticulously draw on new features
For mere pleasantries.

You want to appear different
But not foreign.
Careful, not too much!
You just want to blend in enough
Not to raise suspicion.
If you do come into any trouble,
You will have to tranquilize
Your natural instinct to run.
You're all done!
Now...look in the mirror.

Me:
What the –

Destiny:
I know it's different and not you,
But it will keep you safe.

Me:
I don't like it.
Why do I have to wear this?
Why can't I just be me?
I don't wanna wear this thing.
I look like a fool.

Destiny:
You don't look like a fool.
Can you wear it for now?
Soon, it will all make sense.

Me:
Ugh...okay...I guess.

Destiny:
Don't worry.
I'll be right there with you.

THE AMERIKIN DREAM

When I was a boy,
I heard stories about it.
When I was a teenager,
I thought about it.
When I was a young man,
I went looking for it.
I crossed state lines,
I stepped about unwelcoming territories,
I crawled out of doubt,
I hiked up mountains of mistakes,
I tiptoed across unequal standards,
I swam in a sea of tears,
I walked through fields of failure,
I stumbled over doubt
But had no luck.
Then one day during
A moment of life's misfortune,
As I laid in defeat,
As I cried for resolve,
As I clung to hope –
Something appeared.
Upon closer look,
I saw standing before me
A reanimated belief assembled
From what appeared to be scraps
Of prosperity left behind
By previous generations.
A grotesque lie barely held together.
A concept that had been maimed
By corporate greed and selfish pursuits
Of pleasures for money over public welfare.
A half-dead idea with no soul,
Predatorily staring back at me,
Ready to rip me apart.
Startled, I stepped back in fear.
It was a monster!
It slipped on a rock of uncertainty.
It appeared afraid.
It seemed hurt.
It looked as if it needed my help.

I will step forward.
I will tend to its wounds.
I will tame it.
I will train it.
I will rescue it.

I will find who did this.

SECRET BEHIND THE MASK

I
try
to leave
it trapped inside,
hoping my true
self is disguised
by wrapping it
in a small cocoon,

but it's bound to come out soon.

But
I can't
let the
real me show.
Destiny said not
everyone can know.

I have to keep "me" concealed
until it's safe to remove this mask
and allow my identity to be revealed.

BITTEN BY JUDGMENT

I pull at your conscience
   by wrapping hurtful words
      around the tip of your tongue,
      like clenching at my prey,
   and won't let go until your words
become a silhouette of what you say.

I am a decoy waiting to engage
   on any unknown targets −
      to engulf their confidence
      into poisonous flames and
   sting any remaining self-esteem
with venom lying within my fangs.

And when my work here is done,
   I slither across the ground, creating
      zigzag prints across the surface of
      the sand like hateful words ice skating
   on a blank canvas leaving a mess behind,
then shed my skin before you realize:
You.
   Are.
      Bit.

ALL IT TOOK WAS SOMEBODY'S WORD

All

it took was

somebody's word

for me to get a lower grade

than what I knew I really deserved;

for me to graduate, get a job, and get fired;

for me to have my health and livelihood ruined;

for me to have to sleep on trains and bathe at gyms;

for me to be blamed and called a nigger from the hood;

for me to choose between justice and new opportunities

but make the wrong decision, and it all happened again;

for me to question my worth and ask myself, *Who am I*;

for me to turn myself in and be walked in handcuffs;

for my degrees, my awards, my achievements,

and my own word not to mean anything;

for the details to really not matter

because for it all to happen

again, all it takes is

somebody's

word.

TWO ATTORNEYS

I sat alone on my half-blown airbed
With frustration feeding on my head.

Prejudice stole almost all the money I saved,
Keeping my American Dream enslaved.

I used what was left to retain two attorneys
To calm my anxiety and worries.

They both charged me a high retainer fee,
But one worked mainly on contingency.

One was needed just for show,
And one was just for the parties involved to know.

One I hired to protect my reputation,
And one to close a sham investigation.

One to help me find peace,
And one to answer questions from the police.

One to make them pay,
And one to not let them take my freedom away.

One was just plain rude,
And one cheered me on: "They are all screwed!"

One I never actually met,
And one mailed them a letter as a threat.

One sent his associate to stand beside me,
And one pressured me to sign and agree.

One I told, "You're doing my case a disservice."
And I thanked him for his service.

Then, another one I had to hire
To replace the one with little desire...

God...this is absurd!
All this drama because of somebody's word!

WHAT WOULD YOUR PRICE BE?

Have you ever had
to write your own
survival guide
to homelessness?

Carry around town
your dignity
and all you had
in a bag

on your back?
Been asked to auction
your emotional distress?
Been left with a

bullet Prejudice put
in your head?
Calculate the value
of your suffering?

Appraise the worth
of your tears
and slashes they left
down your face

from being hated
because of your race?
Come up with a figure
that matched your pain?

If you had to,
what would
your price
be?

THE PLEDGE

How can I pledge allegiance
to the Flag of
the United States of America
or to the Republic
for which it stands
when our nation is divided
with brutalities and injustices
for people who look like me?

THE CLOSING ARGUMENT

Good evening, Your Honor,

Ladies and gentlemen of the jury,

Thank you for your participation.

This was a long trial about insensitivity
With armed robbery of my client's dignity
And an attempted murder of his character,
An experience some have regularly in America.
Now, the defendant pleads agree to disagree
And has proffered a lukewarm apology
With lines read as if at a script rehearsal,
Asked we not take her opinion personal.
On the stand, she wore a smirk across her face,
Making a visible mockery of this case.
Her testimony was a thinly disguised insult
Intended only to sway the final result –
To implant doubt within your psyche
So that you deliberate and sentence her lightly;
To trick you and make you question yourself
By believing evil can live to be something else;
To secretly sedate your intuition
For lesser punishment for her admission.
But remember, we wouldn't be here at the penalty phase
If justice could be served by an "I'm sorry" phrase.
An apology will not excuse what she did.
Remember the evidence that she tried to keep hid,
Remember the intent when she squeezed the trigger,
Remember the shots fired as she called him a nigger,
Remember we are only here because she got caught,
Remember it's only due to a video we have fault,
And remember, the verdict that you will render
Will set a precedent for the future to remember.

The question now is, will you decide to kill Hate,
Or let her live to be America's worst trait?

I rest my case.

FOREGONE CONCLUSION

Instantly,
The verdict crashed head on
With my facial expressions.
For the moment,
My confidence was paralyzed
And the disbelief shattered my face
With open lacerations.
Blood began squirting out the wounds
Of my reflections
On my time and effort wasted.
The confusion dried the moisture
From my contact lenses,
And they formed into rings of glass
That slashed at my eyelids.
The more I blinked,
The deeper the cuts winked.
Shock caused my tongue
To snatch at my tonsils,
And in between this duel,
Intruded my saliva.
This tied up the end of my throat –
I tried to grasp for air
But was overwhelmed with this suffocation.
All I could do was stare.

Immediately,
My soul felt the impact.
For the moment,
My spirit was ruined.
Sharp, spiked needles arose on my arms –
They were chill bumps
But felt like thorns.
Every bone in my body began to crack,
And my skin started peeling
Like ashes burning away from a cigarette.

Suddenly,
My insides began tearing apart.
For the moment,
Defeat tortured my heart.
I rubbed my chest,

But it was too late.
The pain clogged my veins,
Causing them to burst.
My determination was left lying in the dust
Like metal intentionally not oiled to rust.
Then, justice was carried away
In a black hearse.

OUR GLASS

Eternity is a short

time to wait

for equal

rights

if

we are

willing to

stand by for

a change to come.

BACKLASH

My
people,
justice
is a sword.
If you are
going to
hold the
handle,
then you
better
be ready
to take
a cut or
a stab in
the back
from silent
foes – racists
hiding in the shadows:
teaching in our schools, hiring in our offices,
patrolling our streets, and judging our cases.
They are too afraid
to show their
identity
but too
ready to
kill ours.

LIVING RUIN

Prejudice,

You pierced my pride
By throwing darts at my soul.
And with the fingernails of your gossip,
You scratched off my raised mole,
Which was placed on my skin
To play a game called *Rumor*,
Except the rule was I couldn't win.
Then, engraved your signature
To mark the damage you had done
By staining my open wounds
Just to poke fun.

You dissected my complexion
By strapping me to an experimenting table,
But first, you decided the name of my label.
Then, pulled apart my living flesh
As if my skin was mesh
By carving through my tissues
With the sharp knife of your issues.
Then, stabbed me
A final blow to the back
By tossing my remaining body parts
In a bloody sack.

You buried my character
Six feet deep
Under the sole
Of your sweaty palms.
And caged me in a closed casket
That suffocated
Any hope of dying,
Condemning my soul to immortality,
Turning me into a living entity
That lives to suffer with the harsh reality
That I must deal with your misjudging mentality.

So, I await
For the rats to nibble
At my decomposing dignity

And the maggots to feed
On my decaying personality.
And why shouldn't they?
My pride has been pierced,
Complexion dissected,
And character buried.
I have been turned into –
A living ruin.

SILENT DANGER

Deeply buried in the
Subconscious of your mind,
Fragments of regret
From your false police report
Will sit like scattered landmines
And take a lifetime for you
To completely demine.
Silent danger will always be near,
Half-asleep with one eye open,
Waiting to awake and detonate.
Caution will be on the edge
Of every decision you make.
Careful! Try not to step on
Karma's pressure plates.

WORDS MY SKIN CRIES OUT

As I scan deep within for clarity,
I am confronted by my inner identity –
It cries out to me,

My texture is hatred's meal
Set aside for society to peel.
And my flesh the world doesn't accept;
It kills,
Kills heavier than the hand
That squashes a fly hanging on the wall,
Wall for my spirit to slide down
Like a teardrop and fall,
Fall to lie on the ground to be absorbed –
Any moisture will surely be destroyed,
Destroyed like the prisoner's soul
During the moment of execution –
O America, my unrequited love,
I would have lived giving to this country,
And I would have died knowing
That, after generations,
You see my economic value
As my life's only contribution.

PENDULUM SWINGS

Activism is trendy
      when the elite
      can weave it
          with capitalism.

          You just wait and see
      what happens when
      the pendulum swings
back to conformity.

WHEN THEY SERVE YOU DISRESPECT

When they serve you disrespect
and offer you leftovers
or food scraps
collected from their last dignity feast,
you have to know
when to get up from the table,
when to have a food fight,
when to dismiss them,
when to change seats,
when to reset the utensils,
when to order something else,
when to take a bite just to spit it out in their face,
when to throw it in the trash,
and when to flip the table
and make it be everybody's last supper!

WORDS TO A RACIST

Warning:
    Don't go diving so deep
    into disinformation
        that you drown
      in self-deception.
          Even when there
        is evidence thrown
            in for you to hold on to,
          you choose to
            grab on to hate.

              Death by ignorance
         is an avoidable fate

    if you reach for the truth,

hold on to the facts,

        and let go of your biases.

FREE YOUR SPEECH

You are free to
    free your speech,
        but the facts
            will still be true.

You are free to
    free your speech,
        but my rebuttal
            will come after you.

You are free to
    free your speech,
        but just know, I
            will free mine too.

TO PULL A FOOL OUT OF STUPIDITY

To   pull

    a fool

                  out
                    of
                        stupidity,

you   will   have

            to
             be   willing

to

            step
                 into
                    the   mess

      with   him –
slide in lies
                    muddied

                              as alternative facts,
                      trade insults

      as freedom of speech,

and

            soak in

    hate

                as patriotism.

KILLING GOSSIP

Enter.

By the ending of this poem,
I hope your skin becomes scorched
From the steam of these burning words,
Consisting of my ascending agitation
And my flaming frustration
That has reached its boiling point.

Sometimes I envision
Slinging you over the highest mountain,
Throwing your dignity
In between the sun and the horizon
Where it will suffer for eternity,
Pushing you over an open pit
Full of shattered glass
Just to grin at the backlash
That your flesh will face
From the sharp, thrusting slash,
Tying a leash tight around your neck
To command you,
Train you,
And teach you my tricks.
And if you get them wrong,
I'll yank at the collar
Before you have any time
To reflect or holler.

Sometimes I imagine
Holding your head of regret
Under my dirty bath water,
Drowning all of your rumors,
And then leaving them floating,
Slashing a machete at your head
Just to watch it hover
Through the air like confetti.

Sometimes I think
About sewing together your eyelids,
Sealing your lips shut,
And backstitching fabric over your face.

Because why should anyone
Have to look at such an ugly disgrace?

Sometimes I fantasize
About making you sniff black pepper.
Smell the aroma.
Doesn't it smell tasty?
Then, try some salt –
Inhale the spices of my distraught!
About forcing you to sip
The juice of your astonishment,
Gulp your embarrassment,
Swallow it down for further harassment.
About freezing your hatred with my success,
Then setting fire to your ignorance
With the fuel of my perseverance.

Sometimes I daydream
About dragging your hair of regret
Into my dimension
Where I control the vertical
And the horizonal,
Then tattooing these words,
Which are too close to voodoo,
To the top of your dome
So you can market my name.
You are my new product
That will bring me fortune and fame.
About repeatedly slamming your fingers
In the door of my rage,
And don't cry,
Maybe next time you will learn to act your age.

Before I conclude,
I force you into a pitch-black narrow cell
And have no mercy
As I slap your hate around,
Until it stumbles to the ground.
Then kick your apology in the gut
With the size eleven
Of my right foot.

Exit.

ME IN A MEMORY

We are living alone together,
Self-contained beings
Searching for "me."

We are free to proclaim,
"This is me!"
But what if the world disagrees?

We can protest
And just be!
But what if they choose not to see?

Then, do we live as a mystery?
Or give them a fantasy
And hide "me" in a memory?

LETTER I LEFT FEAR

You forgave my cheating
With your fraternal twin, Courage;
Held me captive
By your best friend, Anxiety;
Locked me up in a dark dungeon;
Controlled the terms
Of this forced agreement;
Let me out only
To go to that job I hated
Because you knew my punishment
Would be a low wage;
And trapped me inside a feeling too wild
To let out in the open, but limited territory.
Now, I must escape from this love triangle!
As you can see,
I already packed my bags.
Don't worry,
It's not you, it's me.
I outgrew the hope of finding more
Than that last little drop of opportunity
In a pitcher that everyone else
Has already drank from.
But I must confess,
You were my wall,
And I was the picture that hung on you.
Our crutch was a nail,
The bridge uniting this connection.
I will miss the way
You quietly tip-toed around my heart,
Parading through my headquarters
Like a mime performing, using no words,
And acting with your dramatic gestures.
I will never let you decay.
My sweet tooth will forever crave
To be fed the purest of challenges
And the bittersweet taste
Of learning from mistakes.
Still, bae, I must runaway.
I would rather try and fail
Than remain trapped in the lies you tell.
I am leaving you to just be me.

WHAT

I WANT

THEM TO

SEE

PART III

HIERARCHY OF NEEDS

I
am me,
an American,

a human being demanding
equal rights and civil liberties,
respect, and acceptance from others.

I belong. I am worthy of love, trust, intimacy,
and relationships. I can give and receive affection.

I should be able to live a life free from discrimination where

people like me have access to adequate housing, food, and health care.

OVERINDULGENCE

No modifier may alter my feelings.
Every since you presented your bare complexion,
I have craved to devour your sweet definition
And consume all your pure concentration
Until I feed this starving obsession.
Words may only entice my emotions.
I can taste the meaning as I write
But only a spoonful of phrases
Have been left for me to copyright.
This famine tantalizes my taste buds
And criticizes my temptation.
Simply smelling your earthy aroma
Sends me to a coma.

No tense can fulfill this burning sensation.
Without L and E,
IF will be left lingering to my life.
The absence of your presence
Will abbreviate my soul as it takes
And aggravate my heart as it breaks.
I cannot escape.
I am ranging further away
From my boundaries.
I am becoming absorbent
To you like a clone.
I just hope my happiness will not
Be blown about while in this cyclone.

No punctuation mark may interrupt our bond.
Two brackets,
Love and admiration,
Have tenderly enclosed me
In this habitual inclination.
And as I scan deeper into your face,
An exclamation mark
Sparks my expression,
Because your eyes surrender
A vulnerable distinction.
It is a smear
My spirit will never
Be able to fully erase.

MIRAGE

How
shall I
project such a
strained vision when
the glare of which I stare
at really isn't there? A vacant
desire hovers over my pale mind.
Fantasy and reality are entwined.
Perfection in sight is so distant from
my touch. Yet, affection deep in my heart
is near enough to clutch. An illusion so genuine
secretly portrays false emotions as such. How can a
picture so vivid display vague imagery? And imaginary

whispers speak in detail true lies? If only my eyes could

glow, maybe then the gestures I scan would confess all
there is my heart desires for you to know. How shall I
illustrate such a constrained concept when as I write,
phrases decay as the transition from night and day?
This feeling is like light escaping underneath the
door crack. Desperate desires develop false
impressions, and intense emotions echo
silent expressions. A faint shadow
forever lingers over my heart,
but exposing such an
illusion will separate
you and me
apart.

SOLAR ECLIPSE

If only you could see things from my vantage.
I am suffering permanent retina damage
And blindly mesmerized during this brief glimpse
From staring directly at your solar eclipse.
Words may only provide you with a vague hint
To how I feel watching this celestial event,
Anxiously contemplating what I shall declare
But unwillingly struck by your bright glare.
Uncertainty has been my heart's hesitation
As I view different stages of this rare formation.

Reluctantly, I ponder acting upon this subtle glance
Instead of being bedazzled in a romantic trance.
The side effects from this viewing are still unknown,
But my proposition for thee I will no longer postpone.
You had my attention ever since the very first sight,
And your radiance has been my day's highlight.
So while the Earth, Moon, and Sun align,
I shall respectfully ask, will you be my mine?
Patiently, I will be waiting, anticipating your reply
As I stare once more up at the sky.

THE INVESTMENT

I'm invested in a portfolio of love,
Risking feelings that I can't get rid of.
So pooled in a financial institution,
Paying all to a mutual contribution.
Anxious for interest to accumulate
But trying not to overestimate.
Strategically, I purchase each share,
Increasing ownership in this affair.
Desire has put me so close to debt,
Bidding on emotions I've never felt.
There's something about this bond
Making me feel obligated to fund.
For I would deposit my last dime,
Betting on your heart for a lifetime.

THE PRIVATE GALLERY

Come into my private gallery, Love.
The artifacts of my desires are ready to see.
Come into my private gallery, Love.
I recovered precious objects to share with thee,
And custom mounted each fragile piece
On an armature of faith retrieved from life's debris.

Displayed beyond the hallway, you will find
A soft spot sealed in the chambers of my mind,
And a thought-filled hourglass
That is romantically calibrated to a morass.
For I am drifting to a fantasy in reality
Unaware of time trickling me closer to mortality.

Splattered about the next room
Are specks of suppressed feelings that loom.
Each dot marks my heart's dissent
From spilling affection without my consent.
So to freely let the emotions rain,
I built this space for the passion to drain.

Hung in the next area we will walk through,
Are large canvases painted red, yellow, and blue.
My choice of using these primary colors
Is to represent my lack of interest in the "others."
Over half a decade, you have been my crush –
The only medium that has inspired my paintbrush.

Preserved records kept in the archive
Reveal a question that I can no longer deprive.
For many years I have sought
To finally remove this ring from the vault,
Then get down on one knee
And formally ask,

Will you marry me?

THE SAID, UNSAID

My Love,
What is it you want from me?
The gestures of my heart
Cannot understand the expression
Of your body's silent remark.
When I try to walk away,
You grab my hope and say, "Stay."
When I ask you to make a choice,
Confusion cracks your voice.
When I ask if I should resist,
Why do your eyes
Encourage me to persist?
What is it that you want from me?
What are you not telling me?

THIS IS IT, YOU ARE FREE

This thing, love, is more than just a word.
Not a weapon to be drawn out as a sword.
Satisfaction has only crept in throughout the years
With lust whispering empty promises in my ears.
And we know this tiptoeing will not last,
      Because I cannot make you love me
As your beloved from a long-lost, unforgotten past;
      So, I'll let you go. Now, you are free.

There is an outbreak of my optimistic thinking,
And my heart is plagued due to our past reprinting.
But we are over, and I will crumble every bit of hope;
No ties to each other; this time, I will just have to cope.
How is it the unsaid said a great deal to reality,
      And the truth arose from the debris,
But still, your lies could remain with totality?
      So, I'll let you go. Now, you are free.

I never knew that a kind lie could be so cruel,
And the subtle truth would be my heart's duel.
I was forgiving, and you took my trust like a thief,
Repeatedly returning, forming an elaborate motif.
Oh, so creative the way you spun your web of deceit,
      Then deviously tangled me with glee
And wrapped my eyes so that you could cheat;
      So, I'll let you go. Now, you are free.

Our relationship can never maintain mass.
We are as explosive as flammable gas.
Together, our energies cause conflict to ignite –
Mainly due to the past that you want to reunite.
And the scent of your unfaithfulness is so distinct,
      Similar to the smell of a Ginkgo tree.
Over time, it caused your promises to become extinct;
      So, this is it. You are free.

'TIL DEATH DO US

Forever
would have
been
worth the
wait.

And I
would have
loved to left
"forever" playing
on a loop.

Faithfully
yours,
'til
death
do us.

THE FELON

When you are born into neglect,
The presumption of innocence
Will not apply to you.
You will be wrongfully convicted
For your parents' crimes
And sentenced to serve a lifetime
Facing social stigma
In solitary confinement,
Caged in a cell of circumstance.
You will be held accountable for their mistakes
And receive punishment for their failures.
You will be unable to appeal
This transgenerational inheritance.
Parole will only be granted
If you can prove your worth.
They will appraise your intrinsic value
Through a lens of preconceived opinions
About your emotional intelligence,
Estimate possible commitment issues,
Then decide if you are a low risk for release.
They will ask, if freed, how can you be trusted
To obediently participate in society.
They will analyze your responses to determine
Whether you are capable of breaking
An intergenerational cycle of incarceration,
Or if you will likely be a repeat offender.
You will have to convince them
You have taken responsibility
For crimes you did not commit
And have been fully rehabilitated.
But if they give you freedom,
You will then have to reassure the world
That you are more than just an ex-convict.
But the label will be permanently attached
To you like a scarlet letter.
Your past will be a red flag to everyone else.
You will need to make a persuasive argument
For them to believe you chose nature over nurture.

A BLANK PAGE

A blank page

is as cold

as a corpse –

full of opportunity

for me to breathe life

into a body of work

or cremate dead relationships

and let the words flow

from the urn

like   ashes   sprinkled

        in   the   wind

                        as   I   pay

                    my   last

                                        respects.

CREMATORIUM

Staring down at your cold corpse
Makes me question how life works.
I really cannot understand how
A few moments from now
You will be put into a vase –
It brings rain down my face.
If I could give my life to borrow,
I would just to get past the sorrow.

Grieving your sudden absence
Takes a great deal of acceptance.
I am still infused with confusion.
Is this really our conclusion?
All at once, everything just ceased –
No time for me to prepare at least.
How can I lay you down to rest
When we were each other's best?

Knowing that you cannot reply
Makes it harder to say goodbye.
So many words I never got to utter –
They will just be melted like butter.
Although your spirit may be near,
This message your body cannot hear.
Everything could just be back the same
If you awake before they start the flame.

Thinking about seeing your body burn
Means dealing with filling this empty urn.
I have been saddened by the exclusion –
This condemned state of forced seclusion.
Pain is my only friend now that you're gone,
And my head sits on its shoulders like a stone.
They have already started to turn up the heat.
I will miss you, Love, each day, until we meet.

CREMATORIUM PREQUEL

After she was delivered the sad, tragic news,
Dejection stayed on her face like a bruise.
For three full days, despair and she just slept,
Soaking in the puddle of tears that she wept.
The grief on her plush pillow formed a stain,
And anger spilled on the cushion of her pain.

During the subsequent stages of her mourning,
Rage would overtake her without forewarning.
The initial shock still pumped through her veins.
She just couldn't picture looking at his remains.
They had just celebrated their fifth anniversary
And now life without him would be a mystery.

As soon as the day arrived to give her farewell,
Missing him was all that her mind could dwell.
She glanced at the artworks that he had painted
And, by God, at that moment, she almost fainted.
The images he drew made her memories roam
Throughout her slow ride to the funeral home.

Before she entered the room, she dried her face.
Her body language, though still, remained at bass.
The undertaker offered her his silk handkerchief,
But it seemed as if her consciousness was adrift.
She just stared right at his body for a short while.
Then, without warning, she released a painful howl.

When she finally accepted that he was deceased,
She requested some time to speak with the priest
And explained not being sure how to let go –
It was a lot she wanted her dearly beloved to know.
Seeing her uncertainty of the exact words to say,
He suggested letting them come out as they may.

THE APPRAISAL

Mama,

Being raised in a dysfunctional family,
Primed me to imperfect conditions
Necessary to cast a gold metal ring
And perfectly set ambition on a dream
For marriage and a family of my own.
I grew up managing the pressures of life
Without you, and created a diamond
Using hope and craftsmanship,
Coupled with careful attention to
Courage, resilience, and perseverance.
I made a vow to myself that your neglect
Would not be a pretext for my failure.
No matter how unfair the circumstances,
I would take responsibility for the person
I choose to become and the outcomes
From the choices that I decide to make.
My love potential would be inscribed
With an accumulation of acts of self-work,
Not engraved with childhood adversity.
Hardship to not be a signature of my identity
But a test of who I decide to be in spite of it.

Unfortunately, society has estimated
My value by our relationship,
The connection that was never formed,
A lost bond between a child and mom.
Your negligence has been a devaluation
Of my emotional intelligence
And presumed capability
Of romantic commitment.
It does not matter how bright
The diamond shines, since the metal
Holding it in place is tarnished.
The absence of nurture received from you
Has been an asterisk left for me to explain.
I have chased after Unrequited Love
Because she reminded me of you.
I have watched my success lose its luster.
After almost every win,

It has been you invoked,
"Where is your mom?"

I am judged not by who I am,
But the environment I came from,
And others use you
To appraise the reward
Of being with me.

THE HEIST

Daddy,

The greatest heist ever
is when both your parents
act as co-conspirators
to stealing your childhood
and only leave
invisible bruises
in the vault,
but they pretend
as if the robbery
never happened.

So, when you become an adult,
and they think no one is looking,
they try to break back into your heart
for sentimental fortunes
earned from your life's victories,
but they discover
you have reprinted trust
in a foreign currency,
and the symbol of love
looks unfamiliar now.

"Why?" you ask.

Someone was looking.

I saw your desire
for power organize
a fake marriage
to breach the judge's heart
and grant you a victory –
a prize that was
my life.
You didn't love that woman –
she was just an accessory
to your crime.

I observed your rage
rob my joy when you

removed my awards
off the wall,
packed my trophies
in a dusty box,
and put my belongings
in a bag all because of hearsay
that my mom was plotting
to take your prize.

I heard
your anger
finally break through
as you blurted
that I may not
be your son
with no worry
about the alarm
that you callously
triggered.

I felt the disrespect
and lack of concern
for me
throughout my life.
Remember that time
I wrote you a letter,
and you addressed it
to everyone else
but me,
still!

I watched you runaway
in shame
instead of being a man
and confronting
the blame.
You're no father.
You're a thief.
You stole the trophy
but let it sit
collecting dust.

Why?

IRRESPONSIBILITY

My parents' denial
Is a shortcut to irresponsibility.
A repeated behavior leading
To the same mistake
Is no mistake at all,
It's a habit.
A habit is a personal liability,
Not an obligation for me
To empathize with for exemption
Of individual accountability.
Within every decision is a choice.
Within every choice is reason.
Within reason is consciousness.
Immunity of personal accountability
Is to be on life support of public pity,
Dependent on compassion
To breathe oxygen
Into a self-imposed misery.

THE PLACEBO

Denial is just a temporary remedy,
Self-prescribed to sedate the sorrow,
A placebo to postpone the pain until tomorrow
And pause a recurring childhood memory
From replaying neglect like a melody.
Time moves forward with hurt to follow.
Forgiveness is such a hard pill to swallow
When the excuses provided bring no clarity
Or healing to the emotional injury.
Nor is it an antidote to take away their fault.
Was I not the son that either of them sought?
Where exactly was the paternal instinct?
Their absence has been my life's misery.
To peacefully go on, I'll pretend they are extinct.

MY CONSCIENCE TOLD ME...

An apology short
Of sincerity is simply
A convenient statement
Decorated with kind words –
Disingenuous remorse
Disguised as sympathy
To satisfy their regret,
Not heal my emotional injury.

I SEE YOU

Mama,

As a child, I asked myself,
Where is mommy?
Instead of you being there
for me, you sent Disappointment

to take your place.
And she was punctual!
I could always count on her
being there to tell me,

"She's your mommy,
deal with it." To tell me,
"Boy, she's not thinking
about you!" To tell me,

"Did you really think
she was coming?"
To tell me, "You already
know where she's at."

You sent Disappointment
to take your place.
It's because of you
I know more about her

than I do of you.
It's because of you
every time I see her,
I see you.

NO CLEAR PATH TO FORGIVENESS

There is no clear path

                              To forgiveness.

            One of the hardest decisions in life

Is plotting a healing route

                                    Without a map

            To navigate from pain to peace,

                              So I let mourning guide the way

As a starting point

                  To finding mercy.

THE EXPLOITATION OF FORGIVENESS

Forgiveness void of boundaries
Leaves one vulnerable
To being exploited –
Easily sold by lies,
Deceived by a fantastical possibility
Of moral redemption
Absent of any prior soul searching,
And coerced by social pressure
To remain enslaved
In a transactional
Parent-child relationship.

HEALING

Is healing a journey
You consciously travel along
To a predetermined destination?
Or is it more like a mirror maze?
Do you walk through life
Always seeing the reflection
Of pain around you,
Staring back at you,
Along with what lies behind you
And what awaits in front of you?
Is the only way out
To decipher what is emulated
From a different perspective?
Do you walk by self-love,
Ignoring the distorted images
Surrounding you,
Attempting to deceive you of yourself?
Or do you change your name,
Forget the past,
And pretend to be someone else?

I PUT MEMORIES OF YOU IN A JAR

I put memories of you in a jar,
Vacuum-sealed a lid
On wishful thinking
For changed behavior.

I put memories of you in a jar,
Trapped the yearning
For a genuine apology
And admission of mistakes.

I put memories of you in a jar,
Secured false hopes,
And preserved the disappointment
For a bond never formed.

I put memories of you in a jar,
Wrote your names on it
Labeled as *Parents I Will Never Know*,
And assigned no expiration date.

THE DECEASED

No child wants to lose a parent.
No parent should have to bury a child.
So we buried each other,
Left the relationship unreconciled.
The exact cause of death
Is still open to question,
But probable cause
Is both parents
Showing no affection.
You can still see defense wounds
On their hands and forearms
From defending
Their poor parenting choices
And nonchalantly brushing
Off my concerns
As grudges from the past,
Until I finally hit them
With their lack of effort
Made in the present.
I guess the truth really does hurt
Us all.
Holding on to hope was ripping
My insides apart,
But letting them go
Stopped my heart.
Death freed me from their excuses.
Finally, I can lay Disappointment
Down to rest,
Because God knows
I tried my best!
But I would rather be dead to them
And buried in a casket made from peace
Than remain alive,
Dying from being made
To feel unworthy!

CROSSING OVER

There I am, the person I used to be, lying in a casket made from peace. I haven't fully passed on yet. I'm still in a space between pain and forgiveness. Life without my parents was the last thing I wanted to see. There I am, the person I used to be. It took the passing of our relationship for them to want to see me. But when I said I wanted their attention, I didn't mean me as the centerpiece of a funeral service. They used to always make me nervous, not knowing when my turn was coming. It finally came. There I am, the person I used to be, lying in a blue casket made from peace. It was my favorite color. It's lined in the inside with acceptance and propped up by renewed confidence for them to say goodbye to the child they knew as me. There I am, the person I used to be, lying in a casket made from peace, surrounded by a red rose flower arrangement as a sentimental gesture for our growing estrangement. Regret wrote my obituary. Not taking the time to get to know me will be theirs to bury. Perseverance gave my eulogy, and I must say, it described me beautifully! There I am, the person I used to be, being carried to a hearse to take my remains back to the Universe. There are my expectations being lowered into the ground.

They let me down for the last time.

WHEN THE DEPARTED IS STILL ALIVE

When the departed is still alive,
How do you cope and survive?
There is no prescription for grief,
Nor is time an assurance of relief.
Although the clock is still running,
The hands seem not to be turning.
Days pass by slower than before,
So weeks seem like much more,
And years only continue a cycle
Of pain to carryforward and recycle.

LIFE'S PURPOSE

Who is this creepy, sneaky thing?
It nails me down
On a board of frustration
And hammers tacks
Into my ashy hands' dreams,
Causing them to bleed
Moisture of determination.

What does it want from me?
It has chased my entire
Happiness hot spot locations
And followed my sad spoors
To all their closed destinations.
It has traveled miles through my veins.
Is it seeking to turn me insane?

When will this spinning tornado pursuit end?
Once my joy is plunged into the air of stress?
Once my perseverance is spilled in a big mess?
Or once it catches my stubbornness,
And I realize life is a prey
That should be tightly clenched,
Then devoured by all the willpower I possess?

A BROKEN RELATIONSHIP

What happens to a broken relationship?
Does it fade away
Like scattered human ashes?
Or forever punctures your trust
And leave deep gashes?
Does it hang on like a parasite?
Or is it a brief inconvenience
Like a petty slight?

Maybe it just lingers
Like an unwanted memory.

Or does it become history?

HIS WORDS ON THE LAST NIGHT HE LIVED

Destiny,

I hope
When I die,
It's not from being
Shot in the back,
Hung from a tree,
Or left begging for air with
My neck under someone's knee.

I hope
The world holds on to my legacy
Like a bow and arrow,
And takes aim to my spirit
Into their hearts,
So a part of me
Will never part.

I hope
Memories of me
Rub on my parents
Like vapors to a cloth.
And my passing presence
Attaches to their shirting
Like a spray of fragrance.

I hope
You kiss me on the forehead
Right before my last breath,
And say, I love you,
In a combination
That my ears
Have never heard before.

I hope
When I shed my last tear,
It will be like water dripping
Down a plastic cup.
And that when you wipe it –
It soaks into your skin,
So a part of me will live on in you.

I hope
When I crossover,
My body is embracing yours,
And if a painful death
Be my will,
Then it is done so
Grasping on to you.

A POET'S WILL

When I take my last sip of imagination,
Leave me to suffer with the dehydration.
Continue to pour your heart
Into my words.
Absorb the splash of my creativity
As it spills into a drinking glass.
Consume the dish of my diction.
Leave no crumbs from the pie
And do not waste your water of sigh.
Offer my thirst none.

When my brain receives no oxygen,
Leave me to pass out
On the pause of a comma.
If you palpate my neck
And feel no pulse,
Give me no rescue breaths
Or chest compressions.
Instead, inhale my last suffering
And exhale
Out into the view.

When my pen personifies into a sword
And repeatedly stabs at my flesh,
Watch as the ink gushes from carved incisions
Of letters scarring words that tattoo on my skin
And lines that grow deeper into my tissues
Until the picture of a painful death is painted,
Forming an image
Of a life splattered on blank paper
And creating a collage
Colliding with pasted materials.

When my soul is set free from this life sentence,
Leave my body to rot on my paper's concrete.
Bury my remains six feet under my lines.
Preserve my stanzas,
Which are infused with my legacy,
To all audiences that crave
Their syrupy materials.
And after my spirit departs to that place

Where poems have no defined
Meter, length, or form,

Remember,

I was me, and I was an American.

ACKNOWLEDGEMENTS

When I saw no purpose, and when hope was blindfolded, the Universe, my Higher Self, thank you for sending me inspiration. However, I must say, I wish you hadn't waited until 3AM or when I was on the train with no pen. I'm sure our schedules will be better aligned for, dare I say, book two.

When I planted the seeds, but the words wouldn't blossom, my editor, thank you for your constructive criticism and suggestions. It's because of you this book was able to bloom.

When I dipped vague ideas into a melting pot of possibilities, Dissect Designs, many thanks for taking my concept and making it make sense. You nailed my book cover design!

When stress stacked on my mind like bricks, Thomas, my friend, thank you for constantly reminding me to take a break, get enough sleep, and simply push back the book's deadline until it was how I wanted it to be. I'm a Virgo with a made-up mind, so you already knew I would likely do the complete opposite of what you told me. I also appreciate you for taking the time to read my rough drafts and providing valuable input and recommendations.

When my cries for help squeaked like wet shoes, Vernita, Shanda, Dora, Jacqueline, and all the educators and school administrators out there, thank you for going above and beyond the call of duty to make sure your students are safe and have what they need to learn. You serve as honorary godparents to so many children. Dora, special thanks for introducing me to poetry.

When self-doubt tried to crawl its sneaky way into my head, Ashley, Jeremiah, and Latoya, my siblings, thank you for your support. And thank you to my family, friends, and coworkers for your support in this endeavor.

When my tears burned like acid, my counselor, thank you for helping me properly heal and discover the emotions that inspired many of my poems.

When life gave me those lemons, mom and dad, thanks for showing me, in your own weird way, how to make that lemonade. Though you were the missing ingredients that would have made the taste less bitter, it's because of you that I am the independent man I am today. Thank you for inspiring me to write many of the poems in this book.

ABOUT THE AUTHOR

Kelvin Parker is a poet, fashion designer, and marketer from Little Rock, Arkansas. Poetry is his primary method of self-exploration and expression. His poetry speaks to those that feel forgotten, unimportant, and unheard. The works of W.E.B. Du Bois, Paul Laurence Dunbar, Jay Z, Emily Dickinson, Nas, and others inspire him.

Parker found his way to poetry as a teenager, winning his school district's annual poetry slam. As an undergraduate student at Savannah College of Art and Design (SCAD), Parker started a Poets with Passion Club, created to help students overcome their fear of public speaking and improve their self-esteem. The organization won SCAD's Club of the Year Award and Event of the Year Award during its first year of operation.

The craft of poetry also inspires his career as a fashion designer; he meticulously uses shape and form, color, texture, and patterns for conceptual storytelling. Parker received his BFA in Fashion and MFA in Luxury and Fashion Management from SCAD. He has held various product development and marketing positions with some of the world's leading lifestyle and beauty brands. Currently, he lives and works in the New York tri-state area.

Visit his website for more information at www.authorkelvinparker.com